W9-BYK-552

Discard.

DATE DUE

FEB 0 6 2008	
APR 0 4 2016	

GAYLORD   PRINTED IN U.S.A.

345141 01615   06269B   03

Racing the Iditarod Trail

Racing the Iditarod Trail

by
RUTH CRISMAN

DILLON PRESS
New York

Maxwell Macmillan Canada
Toronto

Maxwell Macmillan International
New York Oxford Singapore Sydney

For Jo, Luna, Dorothy, and Margo

Special thanks to:
Jules Mead: executive director, Iditarod Trail Committee; Joanne Potts: race coordinator, Iditarod Trail Committee; Joe Redington, Sr., and Vi Redington: Knik Kennels; Joe Runyan: Runyan Kennels; Mary Shields: sled dog musher, author; Burt and Ruth Bomhoff: Fireweed and Silver Fox Kennel; Gene Gilman: historian, The Sled Dog Shop, Anchorage

Photo Credits
Front Cover : Jeff Schultz/Alaska Stock Images
Back Cover: Jeff Schultz/Alaska Stock Images
Jeff Schultz/Alaska Stock Images: frontispiece, 6, 20, 23, 28, 32, 36, 38, 43, 48, 50, 55, 58, 64
Steven L. Nelson/Alaska Stock Images: 45
The Anchorage Museum of History and Art: 11, 12, 15

Library of Congress Cataloging-in-Publication Data

Crisman, Ruth.
    Racing the Iditarod Trail / by Ruth Crisman. — 1st. ed.
       p.   cm.
    Includes bibliographical references and index.
    Summary: Describes the annual 1,049-mile sled dog race in Alaska and the dramatic life-or-death event that prompted the Iditarod.
    ISBN 0-87518-523-1
    1. Iditarod Trail Sled Dog Race, Alaska—History—Juvenile literature. 2. Iditarod Trail Sled Dog Race, Alaska—Juvenile literature. 3. Sled dog racing—Alaska—Juvenile literature. 4. Sled dogs—Juvenile literature. [1. Iditarod Trail Sled Dog Race, Alaska. 2. Sled dog racing.] I. Title.
SF440.15.C74 1993
798'.8—dc20   92-25870

Dillon Press   Maxwell Macmillan Canada, Inc.
Macmillan Publishing Company   1200 Eglinton Avenue East
866 Third Avenue   Suite 200
New York, NY 10022   Don Mills, Ontario M3C 3N1

Macmillan Publishing Company is part of the Maxwell Communication Group of Companies.

First edition

Printed in the United States of America

10 9 8 7 6 5 4 3 2 1

Contents

The Iditarod is the richest, longest, most difficult sled dog race of them all.

"I've been thinking about how the Iditarod is much more than a race. It is a celebration of a place, a people, and a sport so unique that it attracts the attention of the whole world."

—**Rick Swenson**, Lightning Bolt Express Kennel,
Pawprint News, February 21, 1992

"I love animals. I love getting out in the wilderness, being close to nature."

—**Mary Shields**, *Have Dog Team Will Travel*

Prologue

They face howling winds, frozen tundra, blinding snowstorms, and even moose attacks. The racing driver and dog team become one as they dare to meet danger together. This is the exciting International Iditarod Sled Dog Race, which covers more than 1,049 miles, from Anchorage to Nome.

In 1925, 20 brave sled dog drivers raced the Iditarod Trail to Nome, carrying precious serum needed to prevent a terrible diphtheria epidemic. This life-and-death race, known as the "Great Race of Mercy," was the inspiration for the modern-day Iditarod.

Today, in the immense state of Alaska, the official sport is sled dog racing. Men and women, boys and girls, enjoy hooking up the dogs, stepping on the sled runners, and racing across Alaska's wilderness. Sled dog racing, however, requires intensive training. Dogs and drivers must learn to work together. Incredible stamina is needed to compete in long-distance races over difficult terrain and often punishing weather conditions.

The longest, hardest, richest racing challenge of all is the Iditarod. Each spring, mushers and sled dog teams from around the world gather in Alaska. Follow the adventures of these exceptional athletes as they strive to win the Iditarod, the "last great race on earth."

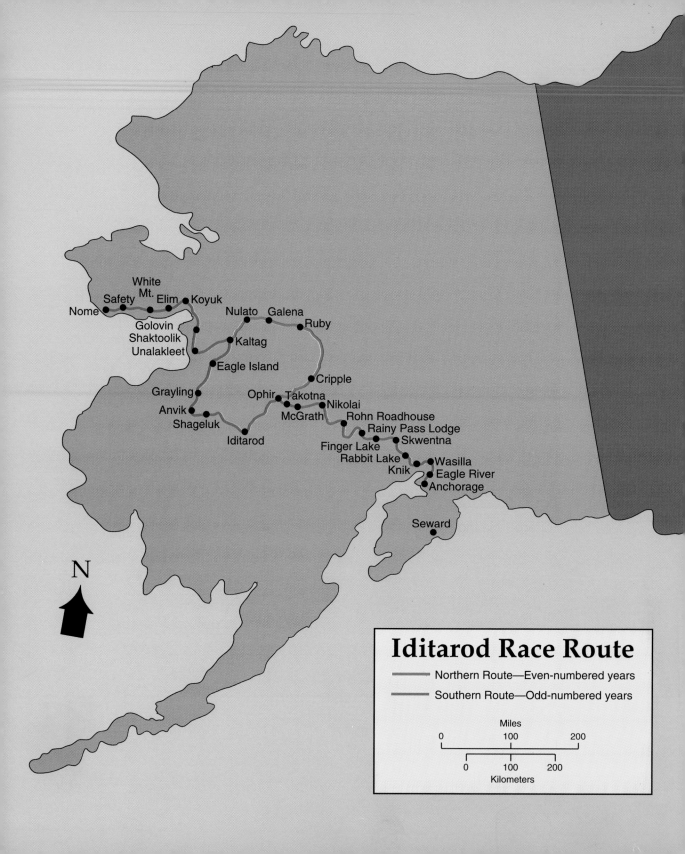

Iditarod Race Route

— Northern Route—Even-numbered years

— Southern Route—Odd-numbered years

Miles
0 — 100 — 200

0 — 100 — 200
Kilometers

N

Nome
Safety
White Mt.
Elim
Koyuk
Golovin
Shaktoolik
Unalakleet
Nulato
Galena
Ruby
Kaltag
Eagle Island
Cripple
Grayling
Ophir
Takotna
Nikolai
Anvik
McGrath
Rohn Roadhouse
Shageluk
Rainy Pass Lodge
Iditarod
Skwentna
Finger Lake
Rabbit Lake
Wasilla
Knik
Eagle River
Anchorage
Seward

Chapter One

The First Great Race to Nome

In the early 1900s a series of trails stretched more than 2,000 miles from the coastal towns of Seward and Knik (kuh-NIK), in the southwest, to Nome in northwestern Alaska. These were trails to the gold strikes, and the only roads to villages, trading posts, and mining camps along the way.

The craze for gold created the trails north as sled dog teams traveled back and forth, transporting people, delivering mail and supplies. When gold was discovered in the Nome area in 1899, the town grew from a few hundred to a booming gold rush city of 20,000 people. In 1908 a gold discovery attracted miners to the Iditarod River near the Athapaskan Indian village of Ingalik. The Ingalik Indians called the river *Haiditarod*, meaning a far and distant place. By 1910 the village of Ingalik turned into a booming gold rush town named Iditarod, and the Iditarod mining district became the third largest in Alaska.

Sled dog teams brought out the gold ore from Iditarod in the winter months. It was not uncommon to see a gold "train," a series of dog teams with 75 dogs and their drivers, transporting 4,000 to 5,000 pounds of gold. In spring, paddle wheel boats from Seward made the trip up to Nome with supplies and back again with gold. By 1914 the gold supply began to dwindle, and by 1920 the town of Iditarod was almost deserted.

But, by then, the Iditarod Trail was established and the sled dog trails opened to Nome. During World War I (1914–1918), the Alaska Railroad was built connecting Seward to Anchorage, 127 miles, and Anchorage to Nenana (nee-NA-na), another 282 miles. The "Nome Mail Train" was a combination of railroad line and sled dog trails that speeded access to Alaska's interior.

Then in January of 1925 two Eskimo children died of a serious illness at the Nome hospital. Dr. Curtis Welch, Nome's only physician, discovered that the cause was diphtheria, an infectious disease known as the "black death." Antitoxin serum was needed immediately, because the hospital's own supply was almost gone. Without it, hundreds in Nome and thousands of natives in the nearby villages would die in a diphtheria epidemic.

But how to get the serum? Nome is a land of snow and ice most of the year. High winds and winter storms blow over the mountain ranges. Planes fly only during the few months of summer. Boats and barges wait on frozen rivers. The temperature can drop to −60°F. With a fierce wind, the temperature can drop to a chill factor of −100°F. The only overland transportation then was by dog sled. The brave mail drivers reached Nome only twice during the winter months.

A call for help was sent by radiotelegraph to the Alaskan cities of Juneau, Anchorage, and Fairbanks. The nearest supply of antitoxin was found in Anchorage. It was just enough to hold back the epidemic until a larger supply could be sent from Seattle, Washington.

In the capital city of Juneau, Governor Scott Bone asked for the best dog team drivers to rush the serum to Nome. The mushers waited

One of the main streets in Nome, Alaska, in the early 1900s. The city was isolated by snow, ice, and fierce storms most of the year

at mail shelters along the route, ready to relay the serum.

And in Nome people anxiously waited for the serum to arrive. It might take 15 days for the sled dog teams to reach them, depending on the weather. The first great race on the Iditarod Trail was about to begin, a race against time, a race that meant life or death.

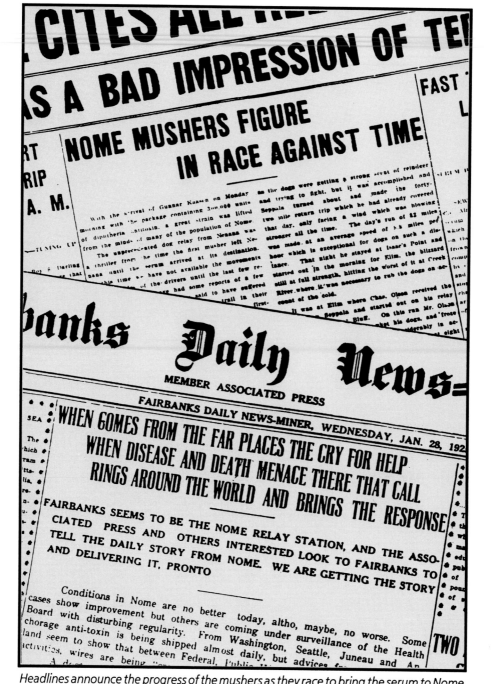

CITES ALL

AS A BAD IMPRESSION OF TE

FAST

NOME MUSHERS FIGURE
IN RACE AGAINST TIME

RT

RIP

A. M.

banks Daily News

MEMBER ASSOCIATED PRESS

FAIRBANKS DAILY NEWS-MINER, WEDNESDAY, JAN. 28, 192

WHEN COMES FROM THE FAR PLACES THE CRY FOR HELP
WHEN DISEASE AND DEATH MENACE THERE THAT CALL
RINGS AROUND THE WORLD AND BRINGS THE RESPONSE

FAIRBANKS SEEMS TO BE THE NOME RELAY STATION, AND THE ASSO-
CIATED PRESS AND OTHERS INTERESTED LOOK TO FAIRBANKS TO
TELL THE DAILY STORY FROM NOME. WE ARE GETTING THE STORY
AND DELIVERING IT, PRONTO

Conditions in Nome are no better today, altho, maybe, no worse. Some
cases show improvement but others are coming under surveillance of the Health
Board with disturbing regularity. From Washington, Seattle, Juneau and Anchorage anti-toxin is being shipped almost daily, but advices f
land seem to show that between Federal, Public
activities, wires are being

TWO

Headlines announce the progress of the mushers as they race to bring the serum to Nome.

12

Some 300,000 units of serum were hurried by train from Anchorage to the end of Alaska's rail line at Nenana. The 20-pound package of antitoxin had been carefully placed in a cylinder, wrapped in an insulating quilt, and tied in canvas. The mushers were instructed to keep the antitoxin warm by the fire so that it would not freeze when they stopped at each outpost.

Beginning on January 27, 1925, 20 mushers with their sled dog teams—mail carriers, trappers, and freighters—transferred the serum from one location to another over 674 miles from Nenana to Nome.

The commissioner of Nome's Board of Health did not know about the relay teams and sent the famous musher, Leonhard Seppala, to intercept the serum package. Seppala selected his 20 best Siberian huskies, with his strong 48-pound Togo as leader. The dog team raced day and night and met driver Henry Ivanoff and his team on the trail, 170 miles from Nome. Seppala took the precious cargo, turned the sled around, and headed for the village of Golovin (GULL-uh-vin) where he was told the next driver waited. To make better time, he cut across Golovin Bay in a raging windstorm with a windchill near −100°F. Seppala's lead dog, Togo, brought them safely across the sea ice in the blinding storm to Golovin.

The next driver, Charlie Olson, carefully placed the serum in his sled bag and continued the relay. Once during his trip the musher was blasted off the trail by the blizzard, but he made it to Bluff and delivered the serum to Gunnar Kaason. There were 53 more miles to go to reach Nome and stop the epidemic.

Kaason mushed on in the storm to Safety, where he reached his replacement, Ed Rohn. As the story goes, Kaason found Rohn asleep. Rather than awaken him, Kaason decided to push his dogs to run the final 22 miles from Safety to Nome. Afterward Nome residents, especially Rohn and Seppala, held hard feelings toward Kaason because of his decision to bypass Ed Rohn.

Upon arriving with the serum, Kaason had received a hero's welcome. Kaason's half-wolf lead dog, Balto, had brought him through the last 53 miles of freezing arctic weather. By a strange coincidence, both Balto and Togo were owned by Seppala. Mushers often loan or lease dogs to each other.

Togo had bravely covered 260 miles of the "Great Race of Mercy." No other sled dog team went more than 53 miles. The effort had left Togo lame, unable to race long distances again. The mercy race to Nome made newspaper headlines around the world. The biggest heroes were Kaason, Seppala, and Seppala's two lead dogs. The reporters called Balto the "greatest racing leader in Alaska" and mistakenly gave the dog credit for Togo's mileage record. Seppala was unhappy with the false reports and knew that Togo was the greater hero.

The courageous mushers had set a world record of less than 6 days (127 ½ hours), arriving on February 2. Besides their pay of about $40, the 20 drivers received medals and certificates of appreciation signed by President Calvin Coolidge.

Today Leonhard Seppala is remembered as a legendary race driver. Over a period of 45 years he won dozens of race titles and covered nearly 250,000 miles by dog team on the Alaska trails.

Seppala's lead dog Togo became part of an exhibit at the Iditarod

Leonhard Seppala, the legendary sled dog racer

Museum in Wasilla, Alaska. In New York City's Central Park, there is a bronze statue honoring Balto, with this inscription:

> DEDICATED TO THE INDOMITABLE SPIRIT OF THE SLED DOGS THAT RELAYED ANTI-TOXIN SIX HUNDRED MILES OVER ROUGH ICE, ACROSS TREACHEROUS WATER, THROUGH ARCTIC BLIZZARDS FROM NENANA TO THE RELIEF OF A STRICKEN NOME IN THE WINTER OF 1925. ENDURANCE—FIDELITY—INTELLIGENCE.

Chapter Two

Origin of the Iditarod

During the gold rush, mines shut down in frigid weather, and the miners stayed at home. Six-year-old George Allan listened to his father argue with friends over who owned the best sled dogs in Nome. A few races had been held in camps and villages, but dog teams were used for work rather than recreation. George wanted to settle the argument, so he organized a race, a seven-mile event for drivers nine years old and under. The town merchants offered prizes for the winners.

While Nome's residents cheered on the boys, George won the race with his three-dog team. Mushing soon became the favorite sport for boys and girls. It was not long before George's father, "Scotty" Allan, got others interested in competing in sled dog races.

In 1907 Nome resident Albert Fink proposed to mushers that the Nome Kennel Club be formed. The Kennel Club members would set standards to improve the strains of Alaskan dogs, monitor their care, and decide on race rules, trails, judges, and awards.

The Nome Kennel Club organized the first Annual Alaska Sweepstakes in 1908, a race from Nome to Candle and back again. The 408-mile course followed a telegraph line, and messages could be relayed back to headquarters throughout the race. This was the start of many formal sled dog races, the beginning of what would become Alaska's most popular sport. Many of the racing rules written then are still in use today in the Iditarod and other sled dog races in the United States and Canada.

By the 1920s airplanes had begun mail delivery service in Alaska. Soon after, snowmobiles replaced dogsleds in the Indian village settlements of the interior region. By the 1930s gold mines had closed and the old Iditarod Trail was no longer needed. By the 1950s and 1960s dog mushing had all but disappeared.

Then two people shared a dream that changed the history of sled dog mushing. The efforts of Dorothy Page and Joe Redington, Sr., rescued the Iditarod Trail and made the Iditarod Race possible.

In 1948 Joe Redington migrated from Pennsylvania to Alaska with his family and settled in Knik, a small town on the old Iditarod Trail. At his Knik Kennels, Redington raised work dogs, and his dog teams served on search-and-rescue missions in the Alaskan mountains.

An Alaskan old-timer had told Redington stories of the sled dog mail carriers, including the mercy race to Nome, and "sold him on mushing." Joe Redington and his wife, Vi, wanted to find the forgotten Iditarod Trail. They searched and began to clear the overgrown portions of it near Knik. Redington not only worked to restore the trail, he also hoped to bring dog mushing back to Alaska. Over the years Redington urged public officials in Congress to make the Iditarod part of the National Historical Trail System. The Iditarod finally became a national historical trail in 1978.

During the 1960s Dorothy Page moved from California to Wasilla, about 45 miles from Anchorage. Page was fascinated by Alaskan history and the sled dog teams that had crossed the wilderness. She wanted to restore the Iditarod Trail and honor the pioneer drivers who had opened the north country to settlers.

As chairperson for the Wasilla-Knik Centennial Committee, Page's job was to organize a celebration for Alaska's Centennial Year in 1967, the hundredth anniversary of America's purchase of Alaska from Russia. What better way than to hold a race event on the Iditarod Trail, a symbol of Alaska's gold rush era!

When Dorothy Page and Joe Redington, Sr., met, they both liked the idea of an Iditarod race. Redington was hopeful, but he knew the race needed big prize money to attract the mushers. The "purse" that he proposed would be $25,000, to be divided among the top 10 or 20 finishers.

The race was set for mid-February 1967. But raising the prize money was a big obstacle. Most people thought the idea would fail. The trail needed a great deal of repair. The members of the Aurora Dog Mushers Club, living in the Knik area, pitched in to open part of it. A big log community hall was restored during the centennial project. Today it is the Knik Museum with a Dog Musher's Hall of Fame and a Canine Hall of Fame.

Joe and Vi Redington donated an acre of land at Flat Horn Lake, just off the old Iditarod Trail, to the fund-raising effort. The acre was split up and sold in square-foot lots for $2 apiece, in later years for $10 apiece. Each lot was numbered, and the buyer received a deed of ownership. As part of the centennial celebration, the Flat Horn Lake land was designated the "Centennial Acre" and preserved as a park. The sale of lots raised $10,000 toward the purse.

In spite of the negative predictions, the first Iditarod race was a great success. Fifty-eight drivers competed in the inaugural Iditarod Trail Seppala Memorial Race, named in honor of legendary musher Leonhard

Seppala. Mushing from Knik to Big Lake, the contestants in the two-day race covered a 28-mile distance each day, or about 56 miles. When total elapsed time was counted, Isaac Okleasik from Teller, Alaska, was declared the winner.

The second Iditarod race was held in 1969, but the purse was smaller than in 1967, and support for the event died. Joe Redington was not easily discouraged, and he planned to make the next race bigger and better. His original idea had been to race to the town of Iditarod, but no one seemed excited about it.

In 1972, during a winter exercise, the U.S. Army helped clear and mark most of the Iditarod Trail. Now the pathway to Nome was opened again. Redington changed plans and decided to race not only to Iditarod but all the way to Nome on the Iditarod Trail. At the race's end Nome residents would be waiting to cheer the dog teams.

But who would race that far over wild and wintery terrain? Most of the previous races had been short distances. Redington had to convince fellow Alaskans that the new Iditarod race would be exciting, challenging, and rewarding. A few mushers who believed in the Nome idea formed the first Iditarod Trail Committee. Letters went out to mushing clubs across Alaska, and excitement for the race began to build. Redington even mushed up and down the streets of Anchorage with his dog team, trying to raise money. His efforts, and those of the committee, raised the prize money to over $50,000, a huge purse in 1973.

The Iditarod Committee set the official distance at 1,049 miles as a symbolic figure. The distance traveled was always more than 1,000 miles, and the added 49 signified Alaska, the 49th state. In March of

1973, 34 mushers started the race at Seward, Alaska, and 22 of them finished at Nome. Dick Wilmarth, an unknown musher from a little Alaskan settlement called Red Devil, won the race in 20 days. Wilmarth's lead dog, Hot Foot, somehow got loose at the end of the race. Wilmarth could not find him in Nome. Later he discovered the amazing husky waiting at home in Red Devil, almost 500 miles away!

There was some trouble after the 1973 race. Redington received letters of protest from Governor Bill Egan and from animal groups, protesting the care of the dogs on the trail. Some dogs died of dehydration and pneumonia. As long-distance sled dog racing continued to grow in popularity, the Iditarod Trail Committee wrote new rules to help mushers improve their dogs' health and nutrition.

For the first few years it was difficult for the Iditarod Committee to raise money. But the mushers were enthusiastic; they wanted to race. In 1975 a large corporation, the Atlantic Richfield Company, sponsored the Iditarod and paid the prize money. Although money problems continued, other sponsors gave financial help, and more and more mushers raced the challenging trail. From its small beginning in 1967, the Iditarod race soon attracted mushers from around the world. The entrants' list doubled by the 1980s, and the prizes multiplied. The mushing community affectionately named Dorothy Page and Joe Redington the "mother" and "father" of the Iditarod for their dedication to sled dog racing.

Chapter Three

Raising Sled Dogs

Most newcomers to the world of sled dog racing buy their dogs, raise them, and train them with the help of other, successful mushers. Sometimes people who want to race will lease a dog team, but drivers know their dogs better when they raise them. The buyer looks for dogs with speed, endurance, and willingness to run. Ever since sled dog racing began, breeders have tried to increase those special characteristics in dogs by crossbreeding.

Centuries ago northern dogs probably developed through crossbreeding with arctic wolves. The Siberian husky and the Samoyed came to North America from Siberia. The Malamute Indians raised the Alaskan malamute, the only purebred native Alaskan dog. The markings on its face look like a mask, and its plumed tail curls over its back. But the Alaskan husky is the mushers' favorite dog of all for running in the race.

Many people confuse the Alaskan husky with the Alaskan malamute, but they are different. The term *husky* is a general term for northern-type dogs of mixed breed. "Alaskan huskies are not recognized as a breed because they are all mongrels. But they're the fastest sled dogs in the world," says breeder and musher Joe Redington, Jr.

Strong pups are the foundation of a successful kennel. A good time to purchase a pup is at five months of age, when the danger of early viral infections is past. A buyer will ask about the dog's breeding and daily routine, observe the puppy's manner of walking, or gait, and also look for signs of any previous injury.

Love is an important part of the training process. Here famous racer and breeder Susan Butcher plays with a pup.

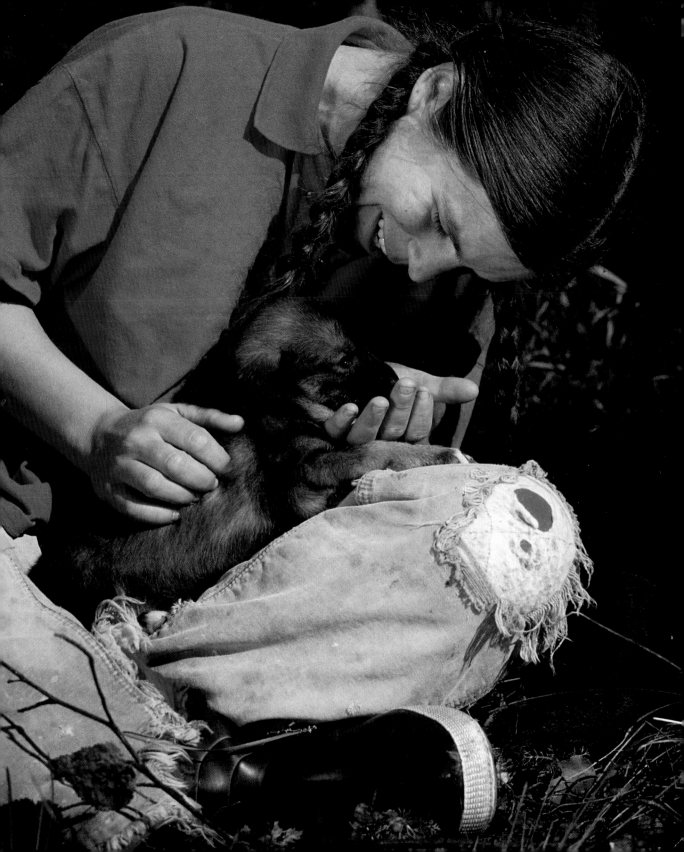

Raising puppies can be a happy, challenging job. It is also a lot of hard work. The young pups are protected, kept in a dry location where they cannot wander during the wet summers or during the cold and freezing winters of Alaska. The pups' mother can visit or stay with the puppies for about 12 weeks.

From time to time the pups are carefully checked to make sure that they are free of disease. The puppies receive rabies shots and vaccinations. At the kennel, records are kept on each dog's activities—lists of food eaten, exercise runs and distances, and behavior.

One important lesson the puppies learn is to socialize, to become friendly. Famous racer and breeder Susan Butcher enjoys working with each pup from the moment it is born in her large kennel of more than 130 dogs. With the help of her handlers, she gives the dogs constant attention and much love. Otherwise they may have problems working with people and the other dogs on the team.

The young dogs must learn how to live in their doghouses and exercise in a small area. After three months each pup begins to wear a collar that is fastened to a swivel chain attached to a pole beside its doghouse. The pups are allowed to roam free part of the time before they are harness-broken and chase the big team during practice runs.

Beginning at around ten months of age the young dogs are taken for walks through the woods and encouraged to jump logs and other obstacles. At about one year of age the younger dogs get a chance to run with the team. A yearling is paired with a well-trained adult dog and learns how it feels to run and pull a sled at the same time. At 18 months the dog is physically developed but not yet mentally prepared for the stress of running in a distance race. By 30 months the dog is considered mature enough to hook up with the big dogs.

Every owner decides on the best method of discipline for each dog. Manners are taught with patience and consistency—no snarling, no biting, no fighting. Around the kennel, a young dog learns what is expected of it and that "no!" means "no!" Treats and much petting and praise are used as rewards to reinforce good behavior. The best way to discipline is without anger, at the time the misdeed happens. Then the dog understands the situation. The other team members learn from the musher's words and actions, too.

On the trail usually all the discipline that is needed is a loud shout or the word *no.* Some drivers find that holding a dog by the nose and giving it a bite on the ear is an effective way to correct bad behavior. This does not upset the rest of the team. Dogs are used to this type of discipline from older dogs in the kennel. A tug on the dog's neckline, a tap with a light willow switch, or a soft hit with a snowball all tell the dog something is wrong with its behavior.

These days, using chains and weapons to hit or scare a dog is no longer tolerated. The Humane Society and the public want to know when dogs are mistreated or lack care.

Dog mushers are educating owners, showing them better methods of raising dogs. Members active in dog mushers' associations, veterinarians' associations, and international clubs often advise dog owners about canine care.

Dogs do not understand many words, so mushers use the same few commands, insisting on correct behavior. *Gee* tells the team leaders to turn right, *haw* to turn left, *all right!* to speed up. Contrary to what is sometimes heard in movies or on television, the command to start is not *mush*. The driver usually shouts "Hike" or "Let's go!"

Sled dogs are trained to run at different speeds. Mushers believe that training rather than genetics determines if a dog excels at short or long distances. In a 30-mile sprint race, a dog needs to lope along using long, easy strides for speed. For a distance of 1,000 miles or more, a dog performs best with a steady trot. These skills are practiced until the dogs run at their best speed for the distance.

Musher Joe Runyan is a multirace winner of both sprint and long-distance races, including the XVIII Iditarod in 1989. At his kennel in Nenana, Alaska, Runyan prepares "a different amount of food and a different number of calories for each dog. Mushers know the importance of good nutrition. Extra pounds on a dog put a strain on the heart and in the long run lead to shoulder and other injuries."

Runyan's lead dog Rambo is a good example of an Alaskan husky. Rambo's type of fur lets the dog breathe when working in the hot weather, and the dog's thick undercoat insulates it during cold temperatures. Huskies lie down and sleep on the snow, or under it with their noses out, and stay quite warm. Between their toe pads are tufts of fur that keep gravel and ice particles from cutting their feet. Their strong bodies run well when racing with a heavy load. Runyon says, "One great leader makes all the difference in winning a race."

Chapter Four

What Makes a Winning Team?

Serious training for the dogs begins after the summer months. The leaves turn fall colors and the temperature drops to 30°F at night. Snow is on the way. The sled dogs welcome the energizing winter weather. At the kennel, excitement reigns. The huskies are barking and jumping as the owner and handler walk around the yard and select the team. In the *gang hitch*, each dog is unhooked from its post, held by the collar, and quickly walked over to the sled. One at a time, the huskies are attached to the *gang line*, side by side.

Each dog has its job. The *lead dogs* are first in line and must follow the trail and obey the musher's commands. The rest of the dogs are lined up in pairs, behind the leaders. The *swing dogs* keep the team on the trail when the sled turns, the *team dogs* basically pull, and the *wheel dogs*, hitched in front of the sled, help steer and pull the sled loose if it gets stuck. Eager to run, the dogs strain at their tug lines, howling wildly, tails wagging. Suddenly, at the sound of a voice command, off they go.

The sounds of the driver's voice and a dog's occasional bark mingle with the frosty air. As the team pushes on, the musher hears the swish of runners and feels the sled's movement over the ice and snow. With a different command, the dogs pick up speed and they are on their way again back to the kennel. At the sound of "whoa!" the dog team pulls up and the driver digs the sled brake into the ground.

Susan Butcher trains the young dogs by running them through difficult terrain at different speeds. By year's end the dogs will cover 1,500 miles or more preparing for the Iditarod.

The training continues as the dogs practice different speeds. In a sprint race the dogs take long, easy strides. For a distance race, the dogs perform best with a steady trot. Following the lead dog, the team learns to avoid hazards, stay together on the path, and obey the driver's commands. What if two teams meet? Mushers are courteous and help each other pass.

Imagine a team of 20 dogs rushing down a snowy trail. Nothing stops them but the musher's voice commands and the quick obedience of the lead dogs and team. Mushers talk to their lead dogs, the most important members of the team. The leaders must understand all that is said and guide the team accordingly. It's not always a smooth, safe ride. The driver and dogs face danger on the trail from the weather and the wilderness. Trusting in one another, they become a cooperative team, with the dogs eager to run for their master.

A winning musher knows that training the dogs to the peak of performance comes first for a winning team. Susan Butcher, Rick Swenson, Joe Runyan, Libby Riddles, and most other sled dog racers run their dogs almost every day. A training log is kept, and by the end of the year the dogs and drivers will have covered 1,500 miles or more on the trail, preparing for the Iditarod.

Along with the great amount of physical activity that goes into caring for the dogs, drivers exercise to strengthen their legs, back, arms, and hands. They need great strength to control the sled and dog team when racing.

Beginning drivers, or rookies, mush their dogs on short trips at first. They often travel with an experienced musher to practice skills such as leaning in and out, squatting or pedaling, jumping on and off the sled. To sign up for the Iditarod, rookies must be 18 years old and must qualify by running in an approved race for 200 miles or longer.

In 1977, with the help of Joe Redington, Sr., young people organized the Junior Iditarod for ages 14-18. The young adult drivers train their own teams and race on 130 miles of the Iditarod Trail. Tim Osmar, from Clam Gulch, Alaska, won the Junior Iditarod three times before entering the Iditarod and placing 13th his first time out.

Many people who enter the Iditarod have full-time jobs. The

musher might be a dog breeder, stockbroker, farmer, physician, tour bus driver, rookie, or veteran racer. Some people arrive from the lower 48 states or from England or Europe and lease their dog team to run the event. All have one thing in common—a passion for racing sled dogs.

Unlike most other sports, in dog mushing women and men race on an equal basis. Mary Shields became the first woman musher to finish the Iditarod race in 1973. Since then two women have won the Iditarod: Libby Riddles and Susan Butcher. More and more women mushers compete in the Iditarod race each year.

Race rules are very similar in almost all contests. The teams usually start at intervals of two minutes, and the winner is decided by the total elapsed time from start to finish. The difference in starting times is adjusted for every musher. In the Iditarod, timekeepers make this adjustment at the checkpoint where the musher chooses to take the mandatory 24-hour layover. The musher who left Anchorage last will stay the 24 hours. The next to last musher will stay at the checkpoint 24 hours plus two additional minutes. The checker will continue to add minutes to each musher's time, depending on the team's starting number, before the team can officially leave the checkpoint. This way it is just as if the mushers had all started at the same time, instead of two minutes apart, making the race fair to all.

Beginning in November, the Iditarod drivers have many chances to enter sled dog races. Often mushers sign up for sprints, the speed races, before taking on the longer distances. Races of different distances continue throughout the winter season. The races are not limited to Alaska. They are held in many parts of the United States.

February is the biggest month for sled dog racing events in Alaska. One of the most popular sprint races is the Fur Rendezvous World Championship Sled Dog Race. Each year this three-day event is held in Anchorage during the colorful Fur Rendezvous festival.

Some mushers dream of winning both the 1,000-mile Yukon Quest and the Iditarod, the two longest sled dog races in the world. Considered to be the toughest race, the Yukon Quest begins at the Chena River in Fairbanks and runs to Whitehorse, Yukon Territory, Canada. At this time only Joe Runyan has won both races, but not in the same year.

By late winter most rookies and seasoned mushers alike have trained their dogs and entered racing events. All preparations are completed—food, supplies, equipment are in place. The Iditarod race is about to begin! It's March 1, 1991, and Iditarod fever has taken over Anchorage. The fans are especially excited about this year's race. Susan Butcher and Rick Swenson are the favorites, tied with four Iditarod wins apiece. Each hopes to beat the other to Nome and win a fifth race. With 75 dog sled teams trying to reach the finish line first, who will win?

Chapter Five

Countdown—
Anchorage to Wasilla:
The Iditarod Race Begins

Thousands of people converge on Anchorage, Alaska's largest city, for the exciting start of the 1991 Iditarod race. Within sight of Cook Inlet and the Chugash Mountains, the teams line up close to the starting point at Fourth and D streets. Spectators crowd behind the snow fences along the starting chute, greeting friends and calling out to their favorite mushers.

In Nome the Iditarod Trail Committee will light the "Widow's Lamp" and hang it on Burl Arch, the official finish line, at the same moment the race begins in Anchorage. This tradition began when people at roadhouses along the trail hung out kerosene lanterns to help the freight and mail carriers find their way. The lanterns were not extinguished until the dog teams reached their destinations. When the last musher crosses the finish line, race officials will extinguish the Widow's Lamp, signifying the end of the Iditarod race.

Two days before the race Susan Butcher, Rick Swenson, and the rest of the entrants drew numbers at the mushers' banquet for their race positions. No driver wants to draw either the starting number or the last number in line. The first team out will break trail, and the last team will run on a mushy pathway. Either way is hard on the dogs and slows their progress. Each year, beginning with the Leonhard Seppala Memorial

Surrounded by cheering fans, camera crews, and other dog teams, the sled dogs are nervous and eager to run.

33

Race in 1967, an honorary "number 1" musher has been chosen to commemorate a well-known dog musher, or a nonmusher who has contributed greatly to the sport. In 1991 the late serum runner "Wild Bill" Shannon and the late Dr. Roland Lambert, a sprint ace musher, were honored.

The contestants wear bibs for identification, marked with their number and the name Timberland, currently the race's major sponsor. The names of the mushers' other sponsors appear on their colorful jackets and pants. Timberland designs footwear for subzero temperatures exclusively for Iditarod racers to test each year. Other sponsors include dog food companies, airlines, banks, art galleries, hotels, along with families and friends. Mushers usually need more than one sponsor to help them afford the $25,000 to $30,000 needed to race. Beginners and nonprizewinners often have a hard time finding sponsors.

Participants pay an entrance fee of $1,249 and have the added expense of their dog team, food, supplies, and other equipment. Even with the high cost of competing in the Iditarod, entrants are so enthusiastic about the race that they somehow manage to come up with the money to participate. In 1991 the prize monies awarded to the first 20 finishers amounted to $300,000. The first 20 who crossed the finish line received cash awards, beginning with the winner's $50,000 and decreasing to $4,500. Those mushers finishing in 21st to 60th position received $1,000 each. But mushers feel their biggest reward is completing the distance from Anchorage to Nome.

Before the race begins, veterinarians examine more than 1,200 howling dogs to make sure they are in good physical condition.

Checkers inspect the mushers' sleds for all the required equipment. At race time, officials walk through the five city blocks in the staging area among the crowd of barking and jumping dogs. To identify the dog teams, they mark the dogs with a small amount of paint. Each team is marked with a different color and each dog is painted in a different spot, such as right or left ear, shoulder, or hip. This prevents any musher from switching animals after the veterinarians examine them. On the trail at the checkpoints, no dog can be exchanged for another dog or added to the team. During the race the Iditarod Trail Committee tests the dogs for drugs on a random basis, to assure that the dogs race in a free, natural state.

Surrounded by cheering fans, camera crews, and other dog teams, the sled dogs are nervous and eager to run. Many of the mushers were too excited to get much sleep the night before the big race. They wait for their number to be called, anxious for their teams to leave the commotion in Anchorage. Volunteers and handlers hold the sleds and hang on to the dogs, trying to calm them. The throngs of people press forward but are held back by the fence.

In the midst of the confusion, newspaper and TV crews click their video cameras into position, ready for the big moment. On the street corner at the starting line, mile zero, stands a bronze statue of an Alaskan husky dedicated to all the dog mushers and their heroic dogs.

It's 9:00 A.M. on March 1. The ceremony begins with an announcement of the names of the honorary mushers, the number one position. The official timer counts off the seconds, then a two-minute period of silence is observed—just as if the musher had really taken off. Now the

"Four, three, two, one" and the race begins!

countdown continues, "five, four, three, two, one!" It's rookie Brian O'Donoghue, a reporter from Fairbanks, who takes off in the number two position. One team after another, at two-minute intervals, push off past the noisy crowd, with the spectators clapping and cheering them on. Some of the favorites whizz by—Joe Runyan, number 7; Rick Swenson, number 11; Dee Dee Jonroe, number 21; Martin Buser, number 25. Susan Butcher, in 38th position, kisses her lead dogs, Lightning and Hermit, steps on her sled runners, and races after Swenson. Tim Osmar, number 42, is not far behind.

By noon all the drivers and dogs have left Anchorage. Handlers are required to ride along in the sled basket or travel on a sled tied behind the musher's team, in case of difficulty with the excited dogs on this first stretch out of the city.

Leaving Anchorage takes all of the driver's skill to maneuver the dogs and sled. Hazards appear at street intersections. Vehicle traffic is stopped and cleared when the teams approach. Tunnels, hills, bridges, sharp turns, and boulders may appear suddenly. The dogs have problems adjusting to the city's snow trail. If the weather is unexpectedly warm, there will be stretches of slippery ice water to avoid.

Out of the city, the teams mush about 15 miles of bicycle trails that run north along Glenn Highway to Eagle River, an Anchorage suburb of 25,000 people. The mushers' families and their dog handlers wait with the dog trucks at checkpoint 1, the Veterans of Foreign Wars post. Lavon Barve, number 4, is the first to arrive and first to leave. Soon there's a crowd of dog teams at the holding area.

The dogs are unharnessed and loaded into "dog boxes" on the dog trucks or trailers. The mushers sign in and sign out. With sleds and equipment on top of the dog trucks, the participants drive 34 miles to downtown Wasilla and the airstrip. Because of poor racing conditions the dogs are transported by dog truck on this stretch.

The noise and confusion of Anchorage disappear as the mushers reach Wasilla, a town of 4,000. By afternoon all the teams are reassembled at the airport and the dogs harnessed and ready to leave. The dog teams must leave the Wasilla restart, at mile 49, exactly four hours from the time they left Eagle River. After this no planned assistance is allowed between checkpoints.

Once again the numbers are called, and the race is officially

A sled dog waits in its box to be transported to the town of Wasilla, where the race will resume.

restarted on the long trail to Nome. The spectators wave and shout as the dog teams leave for Knik Lake, the next checkpoint, 14 miles away at mile 63. The town of Knik, population 300, is the home of Joe Redington, Sr.'s Knik Kennels, one of the largest sled dog kennels in the world.

The race drivers will check in and out of Knik Lake. Ahead is the Alaska Range, the Farewell Burn, the frozen coast of the Bering Sea, and Nome. Everything must be waiting for them at the checkpoints. Will all their supplies be there?

Chapter Six

Volunteers Make the Difference

In Anchorage the telephone lines are buzzing at the information center inside the Regal Alaskan Hotel. Race information is also gathered at the Iditarod Trail Committee headquarters in Wasilla, as well as at locations in Fairbanks and Nome. Volunteers call in news of the mushers' progress at every checkpoint. Up-to-date reports arrive at commercial radio stations by telephone and from computer relay systems set up along the route. The location of the mushers can change from hour to hour.

The latest news is also picked up at the trail stops by reporters who interview mushers and send the information to local, statewide, national, and international newspapers. Cable and television stations cover the Iditarod, considered one of the biggest sporting events in the world.

The Iditarod race is run almost totally by volunteers. Thousands of people donate tens of thousands of hours to make the event a success. The "greatest race on earth" could not take place without them. Arriving from many parts of the world, the volunteers pay their own expenses and contribute their time and skills, saving the Iditarod Trail Committee thousands of dollars.

While putting on a race of this size requires many key personnel, there are very few paid positions. A volunteer board of directors represents the Iditarod mushers. Planning and fund-raising for the race go on all year round. In 1991, a total of $2 million was raised at benefits and fairs.

Even the Iditarod "cachets," or officially marked envelopes, are used to raise money. Each musher carries a packet of them in a *cache*, a hidden, safe place, just as the mail drivers carried letters in earlier years. The cachets, marked with the official Iditarod seal, are stamped in Anchorage, and then again in Nome. At the end of the race, the envelopes are autographed by the mushers, then auctioned at the postrace banquet to raise money for the next Iditarod.

Before and during the race, volunteers on snow machines, or "iron dogs," break trail—cut, mark, and pack it. They do their best to ride 8 to 24 hours ahead of the mushers. The crew axes away the branches and clears out anything that might hurt the dogs or tip a sled. With their snow machines the trailbreakers pack a hard snow base that keeps the dogs from floundering in deep snow. But when snow blown by the wind covers the path, the Iditarod racers must break their own trail. Their only guides are four-foot-high markers, painted fluorescent orange on top, that the trailbreakers set up, 12 to a mile.

An Iditarod volunteer for 19 years, Jim Kershner has worked as trailbreaker, race marshal, judge, pilot, and race manager. The race marshal assigns judges to locations on the trail where they watch for safety infractions and make sure that everyone participates fairly. If a team is reported missing on the Iditarod Trail, a plane is sent to look for them.

The race manager puts all the details together to make the race work. It's a monumental task. The Iditarod Trail Committee sends over

1,000 bales of straw to the 20 checkpoints to bed down the dogs when the teams arrive. The mushers' food, the dogs' food, extra clothing, supplies, and food for the volunteers are sent ahead, sometimes by U.S. mail or by the "Iditarod Air Force." This volunteer air force also transports race officials and volunteers from location to location. More than a dozen experienced bush pilots fly their ski planes in Alaska's often extreme winter weather, risking their lives as Iditarod volunteers.

The race manager arranges the locations where mushers and volunteers will stay at the checkpoints, and makes sure that the trail is ready. During the race as many as a third of the dogs are left behind at the check stations, unable to make it to Nome. A volunteer "dropped dog" coordinator feeds and waters the sick dogs, and a veterinarian cares for them until they can be picked up by Iditarod pilots.

The dropped dogs are flown to three hubs—McGrath, Unalakleet, or Galena—where Northern Air Cargo commercial airplanes pick up the sick animals and transport them in comfortable cubicles to either Anchorage or Nome. The dogs are met by the musher's handlers and taken home.

From time to time local students help out as volunteers. Their teachers go along with them and hold classes whenever the student volunteers are not working.

Depending on the location, mushers sleep in town or village community centers, armories, cabins, tents, or zipped up in their sleeping bags out in the open. However, no one gets much sleep. The mushers rest only as long as they need to before pushing on.

The volunteers' main job is to check in every musher when he or she arrives. Before the check-in becomes official, the musher must sign in and give the time, and sign out before leaving. Failure to do so might lead to disqualification from the race.

At each checkpoint along the trail, volunteers look over the contents of the musher's sled bag to make sure that certain required pieces of equipment are there: a cold-weather sleeping bag; an ax with a head weighing at least 1 ¾ pounds and a handle at least 22 inches long; 2 pounds of food per dog and one day's ration of food for the musher; 8 booties for each dog, either on the dog's feet or carried in the sled. The booties cost only about 60 cents each, but the expense adds up since the dogs wear them out quickly on the trail. The musher may put on new booties as many as 1,000 times!

To protect themselves, mushers wear survival clothing made of a waterproof, breathable synthetic fiber. A musher will probably wear an arctic parka, and rules require the use of snowshoes. Extra hats and face masks are packed, along with a complete set of clothes for the coldest possible weather. The mushers wear layers of clothes, depending on the temperature, along with fur mitts and bunny boots—large, insulated rubber boots with studs on the bottom.

With their sleds packed with all necessities, including a cooler and a cooker, the racers are prepared for the worst that can happen. At Knik they leave the roads behind them for the Iditarod Trail into the Alaska wilderness.

A volunteer veterinarian checks the paw of a dropped dog.

Chapter Seven

Racing the Iditarod Trail— Knik to Rohn Roadhouse

Every musher worries about the danger of suddenly running into a moose during the race. A heavy snowfall will force these large animals onto the trail, where it is easier for them to move about. In 1985 Susan Butcher was 115 miles out of Anchorage, between Knik and Skwentna near Rabbit Lake, mushing along with her top team, when without warning a moose attacked the dogs. Butcher had met a moose before that ran through her team, but this one stayed in the middle of them, kicking, slashing, and trampling the dogs.

When musher Duane Halverson caught up with Butcher, the moose charged at him. It took four shots from Halverson's small handgun to kill the 1,500-pound animal. Butcher's team was badly hurt; two of the dogs died and the others had concussions. Butcher took her dogs to the hospital by plane and stayed beside them until the animals could be taken home. The accident to her sled dogs was a terrible blow for the famous musher. It ended the race for her. Now it is mandatory that mushers carry a weapon to protect themselves and their team.

In the 1991 race Joe Garnie, from Teller, Alaska, left Anchorage in 13th position and pulled into Skwentna first, at mile 151. The villagers and reporters crowded around to welcome him. For arriving first, Garnie won the annual Dodge Dash Award and was handed the keys to a new Dodge pickup truck that will be waiting for him at the end of the race.

A moose attack is one of many dangers that mushers and their dog teams must face.

When Rick Swenson, number 11, arrived, he reported that he had rebooted his dogs three times because of the harsh trail from Wasilla to Skwentna. Soon 30 other sled dog drivers, including Butcher, number 38, pulled in and rested their dogs on the frozen Skwentna River.

From Skwentna it's a gradual rise 45 miles up the trail to Finger Lake at mile 196 in the foothills of the Alaska Mountain Range. A trapper's cabin stands there, usually occupied by just two residents. The checkpoint is only a tent camp sitting on ten feet or more of snow. After signing in and out, the sled dog teams swoosh past blue-white woods of birch and spruce, ready for their next challenge—the ascent to Rainy Pass.

About ten miles up the Skwentna River from Finger Lake, the trail turns up the Happy River Valley. The trail has risen only 1,000 feet from sea level in the almost 200 miles from Anchorage. Now the ascent will be steep as the mushers head up Happy River Gorge between the lower peaks of the Alaska Range.

The trail rises another 2,000 feet in the next 20 miles, crossing the treacherous gorge three times, up and down a narrow, winding trail. Going up the steep incline, in 12-foot-deep snow, the mushers push their sleds to lighten the heavy load for the dogs. Each sled weighs around 400 pounds fully loaded with gear and the driver. The dogs can lose interest on any stretch of trail, but on an incline, pulling the heavy weight, they may deviate from the path and slow down. The sight of a small herd of Dall sheep or a flock of ptarmigan can send them flying too fast down the trail. Sleds roll over and dogs tangle on the twisting path. Precious time is lost.

Reaching the Rainy Pass area at 3,190 feet, the mushers see some of the most spectacular scenery in Alaska. The pass is the highest point on the Iditarod Trail and divides south central Alaska and the Interior. The Interior region takes in one-third of the state, reaching north from the crest of the Alaska Range to the crest of the Brooks Range, and west from the Canadian border to where the Athapaskan Indian culture gives way to that of the Eskimo. The checkpoint at mile 226, with a population of two, is located at Rainy Pass Lodge on the Puntilla Lake, in the Teocalli Mountains of the Alaska Range. Outfitters for summer camping trips work out of the lodge and winter some horses there. Two cabins are reserved, one for checkpoint activities and the other for the mushers to rest.

After the climb the mushers arrive at the checkpoint exhausted. At night their headlamps flicker like fireflies as they move around on the broad plateau under a starlit sky. Busy with their customary chores, the mushers feed and bed down the tired dogs on straw. After the dogs are cared for, the mushers check their equipment, then eat and rest. But weather can change rapidly. Once 58 teams were held up at Rainy Pass for four days!

After making it over the pass, the dog teams reach the top portion of Dalzell Gorge on their way to the Rohn checkpoint. The mushers must descend an icy chute that snakes down 3,000 feet over 48 miles on the north side of the range. On the mountainside there's wildlife—moose, sheep, caribou, and ptarmigan. Dalzell Gorge drops a thousand feet in the first five miles, often causing spills over steep inclines. Mushers may not escape without a fall, an overturned sled, or boots filled with water from Dalzell Creek.

The trail crosses from bank to bank in a canyon. Sleds have broken apart and some dogs have been badly injured sliding around the turns. The ocean influence on this side of the mountain has reduced the snowfall. The dogs struggle over hard ground and soft snow. Mushers may come out of the Alaska Range with bruises, cuts, ice burns, or sprains.

It takes great skill to descend icy Dalzell Gorge. Even then mushers may not escape without injury to themselves or their teams.

The checkpoint at Rohn Roadhouse is situated near the place where the South Fork of the Kuskokwim and Taxina rivers meet. The roadhouse, once a stopping place for mail carriers, is gone. A cabin serves as the checkpoint. The Iditarod racers arrive with ice particles clinging to their faces from the raw wind and cold. Dee Dee Jonroe, number 21, led the way into Rohn Roadhouse, followed by Lavon Barve.

The mushers quickly claim their supplies and the large marked bags of dog food that were sent ahead, and take the cooler and cooker off the sled. Food is usually heated on an alcohol-burning stove. For the dogs, dinner might be beaver and fish, with melted snow to drink. Usually the meal is mixed with water, but sometimes it is necessary to insist that the dogs drink water before being fed. On the trail, dogs get sick with the 24-hour flu and dehydration if they do not drink water often.

At the checkpoint the veterinarian examines the dogs, looking in their mouths and checking their paws for cuts and bruises. Mushers are careful to change their dogs' booties often. Once a foot is injured, it doesn't get better by racing, and the dog may have to be dropped. Dropping dogs from the race slows down the musher's speed.

Somewhere on the trail it is required that mushers take a 24-hour layover. In 1991 a mandatory six-hour stop was required when the teams reached White Mountain. Most choose to stop at Rohn, a scenic location. During the race, each musher has a game plan: when to rest, feed, and water the dogs, or when to race day or night against the elements. Most mushers keep a notebook with them, with notations about the different trail sectors gathered from earlier races and practice runs.

If there is sun, the mushers and dogs get warm and tend to overheat with the racing effort. The strategy may be to rest until the weather is cooler to run the dogs. Alaska's unpredictable weather can slow down or even stop the race. Conditions may be so bad that the trailbreakers can't get through. When this happens, 40 dog teams may

Joe Runyan and his team cross an open creek.

be waiting to move out again. For the musher, the delays may mean the difference between winning and losing the race.

Rohn is a transition point from the Alaska Range to the flat land of the Interior, with stands of timber, colder temperatures, and less snowfall. Once the mushers leave Rohn, they must travel the deceiving, windswept area called the Farewell Burn.

Chapter Eight

Nikolai–Iditarod–Anvik

West of the Rohn checkpoint, the teams dodge herds of bison and dangerous river overflow along the South Fork of the Kuskokwim River. In late winter, overflow happens when melted snow trickles into frozen creeks and rivers. Thick river ice extends from top to bottom, leaving nowhere for the snow melt to go, except on top of the ice. This water freezes to the mushers' and dogs' feet, and to the sleds, and hides holes that can swallow a dog or a sled. Along with overflow are patches of slippery glare ice. The trail is moved off the river at places to avoid this.

In contrast to the magnificent scenery of the Alaska Range, the sled dog teams enter the Farewell Burn, a 70-mile-long stretch of barren, desolate landscape. Here a massive wildfire consumed a forest of spruce and willow. There is little regrowth or protection from the wind. It can be a bumpy ride all the way across. Some years there is more bare ground than snow. The musher is often off the sled, running and tipping it to avoid the hummocks. The teams take 14 to 18 hours to cross this treacherous terrain, being careful not to break a leg or a sled. If a musher hits a *berm*, a narrow ledge at the path's edge left by the snow machines, and cracks a runner, the repair must wait until the town of Nikolai (NIK-o-lye) is reached.

Mushers and dogs alike become tired of the lonely landscape. Sometimes mushers see optical illusions. They dodge obstacles, thinking a tall stick is about to hit them in the face, only to discover it's the horizon. After leaving Rohn, top-10 finisher Lavon Barve, number 4, tired under stress and fell asleep on the back of his sled for 30 minutes. His dogs changed course while he slept, and headed back across the Burn toward Rohn.

Ninety-three miles from Rohn the dog teams reach Nikolai, at mile 367. This is the first of the small Interior villages, population 110. Along with a greeting from the volunteers and reporters, the teams are welcomed by the native Athapaskan Indians and their children. The lead mushers check their dogs, feed them, and leave. One or two dogs may be dropped to be cared for by the veterinarian. Some mushers stop and rest, heat bags of frozen food for themselves, or snack on high-energy bars and drinks. Then they go on, the whistling wind whipping their clothes. More than 20 mushers are still within a few hours of the lead. The drivers and dog teams plan on a good run for the next 48 miles. Besides mandatory stops, the mushers usually travel two to four hours and then rest their dog teams.

This trail between Nikolai and the next checkpoint, McGrath, is well traveled by the villagers. Larger than Nikolai, McGrath, at mile 415, has a population of 528. It is located where the Kuskokwim and Takotna rivers come together. Butcher, number 38, checks into McGrath first and will take her 24-hour layover there. Many of the mushers have already completed their 24 hours in Rohn. The rest of the field are spread out as far back as Rainy Pass.

Continuing another 23 miles, the mushers reach Takotna, at mile 438, on the banks of the Takotna River. This tiny village of only 48 natives is well known for giving the mushers one of their biggest welcomes. After they leave Takotna, windblown snow covers the trail and a winter storm from the Bering Sea comes in.

The ghost town of Ophir (OH-fur) lies 38 miles away, at mile 476. Bible-reading prospectors named the town for the lost country of Ophir, the source of King Solomon's gold. At Ophir the Iditarod Trail divides into a northern and a southern route. The race drivers follow the trail to the north in even-numbered years and the southern route in odd-numbered years.

In 1991 the dog teams follow the southern trail another lonely 90 miles to reach another ghost town—Iditarod, at mile 566. This was once a booming gold rush town, but now only a few abandoned buildings are left standing, with old rusted machinery and broken glassware inside.

But silver, not gold, is claimed these days in Iditarod, the official halfway point on the southern route. The musher who arrives first at the halfway point receives the Alascom Award. In subzero temperatures Dee Dee Jonroe and Susan Butcher mushed 80 slow, difficult miles together breaking trail. When Butcher arrived at Iditarod first, she asked to park her dogs unofficially until Jonroe arrived. Butcher wanted to share the halfway prize with her. This became the first time that two mushers had shared the Alascom Award. A prize of specially minted silver ingots worth $3,000 for the winners were poured into a silver goblet and later awarded at the Mushers' Banquet in Nome.

The mushers don't push their teams to win the silver, but they push to win the race. Some say that winning the silver is a jinx. Will it be a jinx for Butcher as she races Swenson for her fifth win? Only once has a musher (Dean Osmar in 1984) won the Alascom Award and gone on to win the Iditarod race.

When the weather gets bad, the race slows down and the teams bunch up at the checkpoints. After 500 or 600 miles, if the trail is fairly open, the four or five teams will begin to emerge as front runners. The dogs are harnessed and ready to chase the "rabbit," the leading musher. Matt Desalernos, number 67, will lead the way into Shageluk (SHAG-a-look), 65 miles away at mile 631. Jeff King is right behind him.

The trail goes up rolling hills and down into creeks and valleys, up and down again. Patience is needed because the snow may be like sugar, grainy with no hard bottom. But close to the Shageluk village the trail improves. Lights can be seen from far away as the mushers come down the mountain into the Innoko River valley.

Now the terrain again becomes *tundra*, the Eskimo word for "nothing." The drivers and sled dogs mush another 25 miles to tiny Anvik, at mile 656, the first checkpoint on the Yukon River. The longest river in Alaska, the Yukon stretches about 1,975 miles from its head-waters in the Yukon Territory of Canada to the Bering Sea at Norton Sound. The Yukon is also the lowest point in the Interior. With cold air coming off the mountains and wind blowing all the time, the trails are hard to find. The mushers meet blizzard conditions as they reach Anvik.

The church bell rang as Jeff King, number 58, entered this scenic village. A special award was waiting for him, the Royal Alaskan hotel's First Musher to the Yukon Award. King enjoyed a seven-course gourmet meal prepared by the Royal Alaskan hotel's executive chef, in the presence of an admiring audience of villagers. After the feast, the winner was presented with $3,500 dollars and a gold pan trophy.

In even-numbered years, when sled dog teams take the northern

A musher drives his team across the "tundra," the Eskimo word for "nothing."

route from Ophir, the Alascom Award of silver ingots is given at the official halfway checkpoint at Cripple. Then the trail continues on to Salatna Crossing and Ruby, where the mushers reach the Yukon River. The first team to reach Ruby receives the First Musher to the Yukon Award.

The Athapaskan residents of Ruby are especially proud of Emmitt Peters, the "Yukon Fox," whose home is in Ruby. For many years Peters has won prize money in the race. He is one of four native Alaskans so far to have won the Iditarod. The other three are Gerald "Jerry" Riley (Nenana), Carl Huntington (Galena), and Dick Wilmarth (Red Devil).

On the northern route from Ruby the trail passes the villages of Galena, Nulato, and Kaltag. At Kaltag the northern and southern trails come together, and the Iditarod Trail continues on to Nome. There is a distance of only ten miles between the two trails. But changing routes each year gives all the native villages a chance to be part of the Iditarod race.

Chapter Nine

Grayling to Golovin

As King dined in Cripple, Susan Butcher fought vicious headwinds, leading the pack into Grayling. She was first out again. The village of Grayling, at mile 674, is the last checkpoint for the mushers until they reach Kaltag, located 130 miles farther up the trail. From Grayling the mushers follow the twists and turns of the mighty Yukon. The deeply frozen river presents another great challenge, curving like a snake through 150 miles of wilderness and monotonous scenery. The temperature here can sometimes drop to −50°F.

Butcher, Jonroe, and a group of mushers behind them were all trying to find the orange trail markers on the tortuous Yukon. Some mushers carry radios or cassette players to help them stay awake and not hallucinate or fall off their sleds. The race grinds to a halt near a small cabin. The next day the leading teams change places several times as they race along the Yukon. At Eagle Island, mile 734, the only checkpoint is a cabin with a few people. Past Eagle Island the run on the Yukon River ends at the Athapaskan village checkpoint of Kaltag, at mile 804.

Lavon Barve (number 4) reaches Kaltag first, followed by Rick Swenson, Susan Butcher, Jeff King, Martin Buser, and Joe Runyan. The mushers pause briefly, only to check in and give the dogs a snack before driving on to Unalakleet (YOU-na-la-kleet). This route connects the Interior's Athapaskan Indians with the coastal Eskimos. The mushers leave the Interior for the coast of the Bering Sea.

For 90 miles the racers mush over the Kaltag Portage on land, a relief from the driving winds of the Yukon River. The dog teams climb a thousand-foot pass, then descend toward the Eskimo village of Unalakleet, at mile 894. Located at the Bering Sea's Norton Sound, Unalakleet is the first Eskimo village the mushers reach. The community of 850 is the largest between Eagle River and Nome on the Iditarod Trail.

In the shadow of Old Woman Mountain, 36 miles from Unalakleet, the mushers stop near a deserted cabin. Lavon Barve had left Kaltag first, but Butcher's dogs were faster and she arrived 45 minutes ahead of Barve. Buser, Osmar, and Swenson followed shortly after. The jam of teams at the checkpoints had slowly diminished, and now Susan Butcher was ready to play the rabbit for the few hundred miles remaining to Nome.

The mushers relax a short while, and wonder how the other teams are doing. Beyond winning, they care what happens to one another. The Eskimos come out to meet them on snowmobiles and form an escort the rest of the way to the Unalakleet checkpoint. There the mushers get the latest race news and ask "Who has left?" "What time?"

The mushers and dog teams rest for the coming ordeal. Here they will lighten the sled load, taking only what they must keep to survive on the trail ahead. At Unalakleet, they are only 270 miles away from the finish line. The wind is up. The temperature, near 25° below zero, is expected to get worse. Sometimes the high winds pile snowdrifts as high as a one-story house! Now the drivers will enter the bitter Bering Sea coast. The snow is different on the coast, heavier because of the salt air.

Nearing the checkpoint at Kaltag, a musher crosses a smooth stretch of land, a relief from the driving winds of the Yukon River.

The trail continues overland for a short distance of 40 miles to the small village of Shaktoolik (shak-TOO-lick), at mile 934. Susan Butcher reaches Shaktoolik first. She has left two of her dogs at Unalakleet, the race has slowed down, and other teams are catching up to her. She pushes on to cross the 58 miles of ice on treacherous Norton Bay to reach Koyuk. Swenson, Buser, and Jonroe are not far behind.

To mark the trail on Norton Bay, Eskimos have chopped holes in the ice and inserted small spruce trees that freeze in place. In 1985, the same year that Susan Butcher had to scratch from the race because of a moose attack, musher Libby Riddles crossed Norton Bay during a violent snowstorm. Coming from behind, Riddles had reached the front runners when she arrived at Unalakleet. Pressing on to Shaktoolik, she arrived during a bad storm.

Riddles made the difficult decision to cross treacherous Norton Bay before dark. Other drivers cautioned that the crossing was impossible, but Riddles believed she could do it. With a new sled packed, the brave musher headed north into a blizzard that gusted winds up to 60 miles an hour and plunged the windchill factor down to −56°F. All Riddles could think about was finding the markers before nightfall.

When she could go no farther, Riddles decided to camp. If she backtracked, the dogs would become discouraged, or "bummed out," and lose their drive to run. Everything she knew about arctic survival must see her through this crisis.

Riddles was frightened at the thought of getting frostbite or life-threatening hypothermia, caused by excessive loss of body heat from exposure to extreme cold. But she managed to change clothes, pull the bag zipper, and keep warm in her thermal sleeping bag. Riddles had given the dogs a snack, and they curled up on the ice, insulated by their fur, tails over their faces. The falling snow covered them and provided extra warmth.

Riddles didn't want to hallucinate. She concentrated on how important it was to win. Ten hours later, there was enough daylight to continue. Following the lead dogs, Axle and Dugan, the team moved along at a steady pace. With one foot on the runner and pushing with the other, Riddles kicked and pedaled to help the team go faster. The amazing dogs fought through the storm and wind, finding markers when their driver was lost, running the remaining miles to Koyuk.

It had taken Riddles 24 hours to cross the 58 miles of Norton Bay to Koyuk, at mile 992. The population of 231 Eskimos was a welcome sight. As the team pulled up, photographers were taking pictures and the crowd surrounded Riddles, asking questions. The courageous woman was now 171 miles from the end of the race at Nome. Her gamble to cross the ice gave her a six-hour lead over the other teams, and she became the first woman to win the International Iditarod Dog Sled Race.

In 1991, while crossing Norton Bay, Butcher, Swenson, Osmar, and Buser took shelter in a cabin between Shaktoolik and Koyuk. Meanwhile, Joe Runyan drove through in about five hours and took the lead.

Most of the remaining trail to Nome leads on land to the west along the southern coastline of the Seward peninsula. The dog teams mush another 48 miles from Koyuk to Elim (EE-lum), at mile 1,040. The village, with a population of 220, is situated on a big hillside that comes down to the ocean. Most mushers are anxious to keep going, so they gear up for Golovin. Over the hills of the Kwiktalik Mountains, 28 miles inland, the trail brings them to Golovin checkpoint. Only 127 villagers live on Golovin Bay, at mile 1,068. The race is heating up as the front runners make their final plans for the run to Nome.

Chapter Ten

White Mountain to Nome

Soon Susan Butcher, followed by the other leading mushers, reaches the small Eskimo village of White Mountain. At mile 1,086, on the banks of the Fish River, White Mountain checkpoint is protected from the wind. It's a good place for the mushers and dogs to rest on their mandatory six-hour stop. One more checkpoint remains at Safety, mile 1,141, followed by a final 22-mile sprint on the beach coast of the Bering Sea to Nome.

Rick Swenson told reporters at White Mountain that although he had the stronger dogs, Susan Butcher would win. Her dogs were faster than his, and she had over an hour's lead on him with only 77 miles left to reach Nome.

In a blizzard that threatened to get worse, Rick Swenson left White Mountain and headed for Nome. Somewhere ahead of him was Susan Butcher. Swenson found her stopped on the trail, inside her sleeping bag. After he passed her, Swenson's headlamp burned out. He tried to change the bulb, in a −90° windchill, but his hands stung and he had to shove them into his snow pants for warmth. Butcher, back on the trail again, pulled up and shone her bright headlamp on his work. Swenson was able to replace the bulb quickly. They decided to look for the trail markers together, taking turns walking in front of the teams. The race was forgotten; now survival was more important. As Swenson started out once more, he turned around to look for Butcher. In the blizzard whiteout he could not see her anywhere. Was Butcher behind or in front of him? He did not know if she had decided to go on to Nome or return to the checkpoint.

Swenson believed he should never turn back, even if he walked the remaining miles. After much more searching for trail markers, he finally found some and a place where the trail turned. He took several necklines (leather straps) from the sled handlebar and laced them together, attaching them to his leaders, Major and Goose. Swenson led the team, walking for hours through the worst storm he had ever experienced. Reaching the top of a ridge, he recognized the location and found a cabin on Topkok Hill. Taking out the coolers and cooker, he fed the dogs, then heated bags of food for himself and dried his soaked clothes. After three hours of rest he started out again into the terrible storm.

Meanwhile, Swiss-born Martin Buser, a top-ten Iditarod finisher several times, had been only hours behind Butcher from early in the race. When Buser saw her heading back to White Mountain, he called that she was going the wrong way. Others had turned back, and the sled dog teams were stacked up at White Mountain.

Noted for his optimism, Buser decided to give it a try. With only Swenson out there in the storm, he had a chance of catching him. Buser followed the scratch marks of the snowmobiles, or "railroad tracks," afraid to turn his head and lose sight of them. And he encouraged his furry companions, especially his lead dog Eleanor. Buser listened to his radio and learned that Swenson had hit not only cold temperatures but raging winds and zero visibility not far from Safety. Buser continued on. He remembered a musher saying, It is not over until it's over. He might pass Swenson.

In Nome crowds of people join the 4,500 residents during the month of March, waiting to see the exciting Iditarod finish. The fire whistle blows when snowmobilers catch sight of a sled dog team. At that signal throngs of well-wishers press against the fences on each side of the winner's chute, trying to catch a glimpse of the approaching team. Who will cross the finish line at Burl Arch first? Will it be Buser or Swenson?

It's Rick Swenson—cold, tired, and jubilant—who runs down the 50-foot-long chute on Front Street alongside his sled dogs to win the 1991 Iditarod Race.

After a nine-year interval, this consistent winner gained his fifth Iditarod victory—$50,000 and a new diesel pickup truck. His time of 12 days, 16 hours, and 34 minutes, was slower than he had hoped for, due to weather conditions. Two hours later, Martin Buser arrived second; the previous year's winner, Susan Butcher, came in third; then came Tim Osmar and Joe Runyan fourth and fifth. In 1990 Butcher had beaten Swenson to the finish line and won the Iditarod. They had started the 1991 race tied, with four Iditarod wins apiece. Now Swenson was one up on her. Butcher congratulated him on his victory.

The mushers had hoped to break the racing record to Nome but this was the year of the storm. The length of time the race takes largely depends on the condition of the trail and the weather. Sometimes the finishers can take as long as 35 days. But no matter how long it takes, people are always waiting to welcome them.

The town of Nome celebrates the Iditarod with many festive events. The Iditarod Trail Committee puts on the Iditarod Awards

Rick Swenson, the winner of the 1991 Iditarod Sled Dog Race, with his lead dogs

banquets, the first one 72 hours after the Iditarod winner arrives. At the ceremony, mushers are given their trophies and checks, and the volunteers are recognized for their efforts in making the race possible. Cameras are clicking once more and the mushers are signing autographs. The committee auctions off dog booties and autographed Iditarod cachets as souvenirs.

Besides the many awards, a flower lei is presented to the winning lead dog and the Golden Harness Award is given to the most outstanding lead dog. Swenson's Major and Goose received both honors. More banquets are given as the dog sled teams continue to arrive, and the mushers are honored as heroes for completing the race.

In 1991, the Timberland Company's Spirit of the Iditarod Award was presented to Joe Redington, Sr. The cut-crystal trophy is given to the person who has best demonstrated the Iditarod ideals: courage, compassion, perseverance, and respect for the wilderness.

Dee Dee Jonroe was selected by the veterinarians to receive the Seppala Humanitarian Award, sponsored by Alaska Airlines. The crystal trophy is given to the Iditarod musher who shows the most humane dog team care throughout the race.

Other awards included the Most Inspirational Musher Award, Rookie of the Year Award, Fastest Time from Anchorage to Eagle River Award, Fastest Time from Safety to Nome Award, Sterling Achievement Award, Arctic Sports Medicine-Human Performance Award, and an Iams Sportsmanship Award.

Brian O'Donoghue, who left Anchorage first, was the last musher across the finish line. Taking almost twice as long to complete the race as the winner, O'Donoghue won the Red Lantern Award from the National Bank of Alaska. The Red Lantern has become an Alaskan tradition, a symbol of stick-to-itiveness in the mushing world.

At the end of the Iditarod race, the mushers are all winners, brave athletes with skill, ability, and determination. They accomplish their goal with the help of champion dogs such as Togo, Balto, Hot Foot, Rambo, Axle, Dugan, Lightning, Hermit, Major, and Goose. Their reward is greater than gold—a bond of love and trust between driver and sled dog on the Iditarod Trail.

Bibliography

Children

Casey, Brigid, and Wendy Haugh. *Sled Dogs*. New York: Dodd, Mead, 1983.

Fichter, George S. *Working Dogs, A First Book*. New York: Franklin Watts, 1979.

Shields, Mary. *Can Dogs Talk?* Fairbanks: Pyrola Publishing, 1991.

Standiford, Natalie. *The Bravest Dog Ever: The True Story of Balto*. New York: Random House, 1989.

Young Adult

Cellura, Dominique. *Travelers of the Cold: Sled Dogs of the Far North*. Bothell: Alaska Northwest Books, 1990.

Dogs of the North. Anchorage: Alaska Geographic Society, 1987.

Jones, Tim. *The Last Great Race*. Seattle: Madrona Publishers, 1982.

Kaynor, Carol, and Mari Hoe-Raitto. *Skijoring, An Introduction to the Sport*. Delta, Alaska: Dragon Press, 1988.

Paulsen, Gary. *Woodsong*. New York: Bradbury Press, 1990.

Riddles, Libby, and Tim Jones. *Race Across Alaska*. Harrisburg, Pa.: Stackpole Books, 1988.

Schultz, Jeff, and Bill Sherwonit. *Iditarod, The Last Great Race*. Bothell, Wash.: Alaska Northwest Books. 1991.

Shields, Mary. *Sled Dog Trails*. Fairbanks: Pyrola Publishing, 1984.

Welch, Jim. *The Speed Mushing Manual*. Eagle River, Alaska: Sirius Publishing, 1989.

Reference Books

The Alaska Almanac, facts about Alaska. Yearly. Alaska Northwest Publishing Company.

The Milepost, a 12-month guidebook. Yearly. Alaska Northwest Books.

Magazines

Alaska Geographic magazine. Quarterly. Alaska Northwest Publishers.

Alaska magazine. Monthly. Alaska Publishing Properties.

Iditarod Runner. Official magazine of the Iditarod Committee.

Mushing magazine. Bimonthly. Stellar Communications.

Maps

Iditarod Trail Map and Guide. 22" x 32". Iditarod Trail Committee. Wasilla, Alaska.

The Iditarod Trail. 16" x 26". Timberland Company. P.O. Box 5050, 11 Merrill Industrial Drive, Hampton, New Hampshire 03842-5050.

The 1992 Iditarod. 22" x 23". The Iams Company. 7250 Poe Avenue, P.O. Box 14597, Dayton, Ohio 45413-0597.

Videotapes

Alaska's Great Race—The Susan Butcher Story. Outdoor Adventure Series Tape #6. 57 min. Seattle: Pal Productions.

Born to Run. Iditarod XVIII: An Alaskan Odyssey 1990. 75 min. Anchorage: Alaska Video Publishing. KTUU, Channel 2.

Gold and Glory. Iditarod XIX 1991. 60 min. Anchorage: Alaska Video Publishing. KTUU, Channel 2.

Iditarod 1989. Second Feature, Iditarod—"The Greatest Race on Earth." Adventure Series. 75 min. Anchorage: Alaska Video Publishing. KTUU, Channel 2.

Joe Runyan, Alaska Iditarod Champion. Pet and Sporting Dog Owners Guide. 40 min. Fairbanks: Snowy Pass.

Season of the Sled Dog. Mary Shields. 60 min. Fairbanks: Pyrola Publishing, 1988.

Sled Dog World. Joe Redington, Sr. 30 min. Anchorage: North Country Films, 1990.

Trail to Gold. The Iditarod History and the 1988 Journey. Adventure Series. 75 min. Anchorage: Alaska Video Publishing. KTUU, Channel 2.

Orders for *Gold and Glory*, *Trail to Gold*, *Season of the Sled Dog*, *Alaska's Great Race—The Susan Butcher Story*, and each year's video of the Iditarod race may be ordered from:

> The Iditarod Trail Committee
> P.O. Box 870800
> Wasilla, Alaska 99687
> 1-800-545-MUSH

Iditarod Winners 1973-1992

Year	First Place Winner	Days	Hrs.	Mins.	Secs.	Prize
1973	Dick Wilmarth	20	00	49	41	$12,000
1974	Carl Huntington	20	15	01	07	$12,000
1975	Emmitt Peters	14	14	43	15	$15,000
1976	Gerald "Jerry" Riley	18	22	58	17	$ 7,200
1977	Rick Swenson	16	16	27	13	$ 9,600
1978	Dick Mackey	14	18	52	24	$12,000
1979	Rick Swenson	15	10	37	47	$12,000
1980	Joe May	14	07	11	51	$12,000
1981	Rick Swenson	12	08	45	02	$24,000
1982	Rick Swenson	16	04	40	10	$24,000
1983	Rick Mackey	12	14	10	44	$24,000
1984	Dean Osmar	12	15	07	33	$24,000
1985	Libby Riddles	18	00	20	17	$50,000
1986	Susan Butcher	11	15	06	00	$50,000
1987	Susan Butcher	11	02	05	13	$50,000
1988	Susan Butcher	11	11	41	40	$30,000
1989	Joe Runyan	11	05	24	34	$50,000
1990	Susan Butcher	11	01	53	23	$50,000
1991	Rick Swenson	12	16	34	39	$50,000
1992	Martin Buser	10	19	17	13	$50,000

1991 Checkpoints and Distances

(Southern Route)

		Total
Anchorage to Eagle River	20 miles	20 miles
Eagle River to Wasilla	29 miles	49 miles
Wasilla to Knik	14 miles	63 miles
Knik to Skwentna	88 miles	151 miles
Skwentna to Finger Lake	45 miles	196 miles
Finger Lake to Rainy Pass	30 miles	226 miles
Rainy Pass to Rohn	48 miles	274 miles
Rohn to Nikolai	93 miles	367 miles
Nikolai to McGrath	48 miles	415 miles
McGrath to Takotna	23 miles	438 miles
Takotna to Ophir	38 miles	476 miles
Ophir to Iditarod	90 miles	566 miles
Iditarod to Shageluk	65 miles	631 miles
Shageluk to Anvik	25 miles	656 miles
Anvik to Grayling	18 miles	674 miles
Grayling to Eagle Island	60 miles	734 miles
Eagle Island to Kaltag	70 miles	804 miles
Kaltag to Unalakleet	90 miles	894 miles
Unlakleet to Shaktoolik	40 miles	934 miles
Shaktoolik to Koyuk	58 miles	992 miles
Koyuk to Elim	48 miles	1040 miles
Elim to Golovin	28 miles	1068 miles
Golovin to White Mountain	18 miles	1086 miles
White Mountain to Safety	55 miles	1141 miles
Safety to Nome	22 miles	1163 miles
	Total	1163 miles

NOTE: The Iditarod race mileage varies from year to year. The Iditarod Trail Committee uses 1,049 as a symbolic figure because the distance is more than 1,000 miles and the 49 signifies Alaska, the 49th state.

Index